Monsters!

Monsters!

Written by Diane Namm

Illustrated by Maxie Chambliss

My First READER

children's press®

A Division of Scholastic Inc.

New York   Toronto   London   Auckland   Sydney
Mexico City   New Delhi   Hong Kong
Danbury, Connecticut

Library of Congress Cataloging-in-Publication Data

Namm, Diane.
  Monsters! / written by Diane Namm ; illustrated by Maxie Chambliss.–
1st American ed.
       p. cm. – (My first reader)
Summary: A little boy counts ten monsters in his room at bedtime but he
is able to get rid of them all.
  ISBN 0-516-22933-8 (lib. bdg.)   0-516-24635-6 (pbk.)
  [1. Monsters–Fiction. 2. Counting. 3. Stories in rhyme.]
I. Chambliss, Maxie, ill. II. Title. III. Series.
  PZ8.3.N27Mo 2003
  [E]–dc21
                                    2003003637

Text © 1990 Nancy Hall, Inc.
Illustrations © 1990 Maxie Chambliss
Published in 2003 by Children's Press
A Division of Scholastic Inc.

1 2 3 4 5 6 7 8 9 10 R 12 11 10 09 08 07 06 05 04 03

Note to Parents and Teachers

Once a reader can recognize and identify the 20 words
used to tell this story, he or she will be able to read successfully
the entire book. These 20 words are repeated throughout the story,
so that young readers will be able to easily recognize
the words and understand their meaning.

The 20 words used in this book are:

at	quick
door	seven
eight	shut
five	six
four	ten
monster	the
monsters	three
more	two
nine	where
one	window

One monster,

two monsters,

three monsters,

four!

9

Where? At the window!

12

Where? At the door!

Five monsters,

six monsters,

15

seven monsters more!

Three at the window!

19

Four at the door!

Eight monsters,

nine monsters,

ten monsters more!

Quick, shut the window!

26

Quick, shut the door!

29

ABOUT THE AUTHOR

Diane Namm is the author of more than twenty-five books for children and young adults. Formerly an editor in New York, Namm freelances for a children's entertainment production company, writes, and lives with her husband and children in Malibu, California.

ABOUT THE ILLUSTRATOR

Maxie Chambliss is the illustrator of more than forty books for children. She lives with her family in Somerville, Massachusetts.